Original title:
The Life in a Pot

Copyright © 2025 Creative Arts Management OÜ
All rights reserved.

Author: William Hawthorne
ISBN HARDBACK: 978-1-80581-869-4
ISBN PAPERBACK: 978-1-80581-396-5
ISBN EBOOK: 978-1-80581-869-4

## Awakening to Green in a Crafted Bowl

In a tiny bowl, green things grow,
Peeking shyly, putting on a show.
A sprout shimmies, takes a bow,
While a bean winks, says, 'Look at me now!'

Fertilizer's a dance of funky smells,
Wiggly worms hide in their shells.
Through laughter, petals wave hello,
As we cheer them on in this lively glow.

## **Whirls of Nature's Tenderness**

A leaf does a jig, oh what a sight,
While soil snickers, feeling quite bright.
Raindrops play tag on the ceramic rim,
As sunshine grins, with a happy whim.

Tiny roots weave tales of cheer,
Tickling the earth, far and near.
Mint goes rogue, a fragrant plan,
While herbs gossip, saying, 'Oh, man!'

## Breaths of Fresh Air in a Minimalist Space

In a pot so sleek, we laugh and pause,
As cacti stick up their prickly claws.
A fern fluffs up, a feathery puff,
Saying, 'This minimalist life is tough!'

Succulent shrugs, saying, 'I'm alright,
Just chilling here, soaking up light.'
A bonsai nods, oh so wise,
Whispering secrets in leafy disguise.

## Adventures in a World of Soil and Seed

Seeds embark on journeys so bold,
In quest of sunshine, warmth, and gold.
A sunflower dreams, reaching for sky,
While peas munch popcorn, oh my, oh my!

Mischief spills from a potted lad,
As herbs trade tales of the seasons they've had.
With a sprinkle of water, a sculptor's art,
Nature giggles, plays her part.

## Echoes of Earth and Water

In a cozy nook, plants play hide and seek,
Roots do the tango, while leaves gently peek.
Sunshine giggles through a window's small frame,
Worms tell jokes, though they're quite hard to name.

Watering can sings a lullaby tune,
As droplets dance like tiny balloons.
Frogs croak laughter from the muddy plain,
While flowers gossip about yesterday's rain.

## Secrets of the Soil

In the dark of the ground, secrets reside,
Where carrots whisper, and radishes hide.
Beetles wear hats made of dirt and decay,
While compost confessions are shared every day.

Mice hold a feast beneath leafy layers,
Sharing cheese tales and their sly little players.
Earthworms are sculptors, they twist and they turn,
Creating great art, while the compost piles churn.

## **Revelations in Earthen Embrace**

In the garden's heart, mischief takes root,
With mushrooms wearing hats made of fruit.
A squirrel composes a nutty old song,
While cabbages nod, cheering all along.

Potatoes peek out, in their jackets of brown,
As turnips roll dice, not caring to frown.
The daisies throw parties, invite all the bugs,
Sipping on dew with their sweet, tiny mugs.

## A Symphony of Sprouts

Little sprouts march in a line with a cheer,
Playing tag 'round the radish, drawing near.
Seeds share their dreams with the sun in the sky,
While daisies dance 'neath a butterfly's fly.

Mushrooms keep rhythm, clapping along,
As vines twist and turn, weaving a song.
A tale of the pot, full of laughter and cheer,
Where nature's great chorus rings loud and clear.

## Hopes Bursting in a Greenhouse Haven

In the greenhouse, dreams take flight,
Tomatoes dance, oh what a sight!
Cucumbers giggle, peas poke fun,
While carrots play hide and seek in the sun.

Lettuce whispers gossip, so light and airy,
While beans dream big, oh so merry!
A sprout yells, 'Look, I'm taller today!'
But the weeds just laugh, 'We'll never go away!'

## Fragrant Tales from Terra's Cradle

Basil tells stories, with a wink and a grin,
While rosemary sighs, 'Let the games begin!"
Chives gossip softly, their voices so sweet,
As thyme joins in, tapping its tiny feet.

A pumpkin rolls over, a big round joker,
Saying, 'I'm the king; just call me "yoker"!"
Everybody chuckles, what a delight,
In the garden's embrace, all feels just right.

## Pots of Gold Amidst the Greenery

In pots of gold, mischief resides,
Plant pals plotting in leafy slides.
A radish wears shades, looking so cool,
While parsley just waves, 'I'm nobody's fool!'

Sunflowers stand tall, thinking they're grand,
While daisies declare, 'Let's start a band!'
They groove in the breeze, oh such a show,
With veggies on rhythm, let's harvest our flow!

## Edges of Wilderness in Urban Spaces

In the city's cracks, wild tales begin,
A dandelion chuckles, 'Where do I fit in?'
With pigeons as judges, cacti take flight,
While thorns giggle softly beneath streetlight.

Funky ferns twirl in their rebel parade,
'Look at us thrive!' the little weeds spade.
Among concrete giants, the plants sing out loud,
'We're here to be funky, we're nature's proud crowd!'

## Glimpses of Life in a Potted Realm

In a plastic home, a sprout does grin,
Calling out for sunlight, let the fun begin.
A cactus tells secrets, oh so prickly wise,
While peas do play tricks, wearing green disguise.

A dancing fern sways to a silent beat,
Befriends the busy ants that march on their feet.
A party of soil, in a quirky mix,
Where roots gossip low, and do silly tricks.

## Exploring the Depths of Verdant Souls

In the land of pots, the stories unfold,
Where basil dreams big, and thyme is bold.
An orchid tells tales of fragrant delight,
While leaves laugh and rustle under the light.

The zucchini preens, it thinks it's a star,
Waving at clouds, 'Look how pretty we are!'
Joking with herbs, both spicy and sweet,
In this leafy ball, they dance on their feet.

## Shades of Nature in Earthy Cauldrons

Peering through soil, a tomato's bright face,
Smiling at sprigs in this cozy space.
A broccoli speaks in a voice so green,
While radishes giggle, their hue quite obscene.

A tangle of roots, like an old pub's charm,
Promising laughter, no need for alarm.
Potatoes tell jokes with a wink and a nod,
While peppers grow rosy, oh, how they applaud!

## Cradled in Nature's Embrace

A tiny green world, where mischief is sown,
Every inch is alive, never alone.
Mint's cheeky whispers spread scents on the breeze,
While beans prank the carrots with swift little tease.

The daisies, like jesters, share giggles and winks,
Playing in sunlight; oh, what fun they think!
In this pot of joy, laughter takes root,
Where every sprout dances, in lazy pursuit.

## Awakening the Silent Seed

In a cozy bowl, a seed would dream,
Wishing for sunlight, a warm beam,
It sighed, 'I'm stuck! I'm quite confined!'
Yet deep inside, it felt so aligned.

With a splash of water, a giggle arose,
'Is this a shower? Oh, I do suppose!'
Roots dance below in a rhythmic spree,
While leaves overhead shout, 'Look at me!'

A little sprout peeks out with a grin,
It chuckles, 'I guess my fun begins!'
'Thanks to my shelter, snug and tight,
I'll stretch my arms and reach for light!'

## A Haven for the Wanderer

In a cheerful bowl, a rogue seed lay,
'Where will I go? Is this where I stay?'
It rolled to the left, then flipped to the right,
Hoping adventure would spring forth tonight.

A friend appeared, a sprightly weed,
Said, 'Stick with me, we'll take the lead!'
With roots entwined, they plotted a scheme,
To conquer the table and live out a dream.

The water poured down, a splashy affair,
'This life is a party, beyond compare!'
They laughed and they danced in the morning sun,
For in this small haven, they had found fun.

## Nurtured Dreams in Earthen Embrace

Beneath the soil, a secret rests,
A dream of sprouting, like all the best.
Whispers of growth travel through the clay,
'Come on, little seed, don't wait, just play!'

The dirt is soft, a comfy bed,
While ants march by, all properly fed.
'This isn't so bad,' the seed would declare,
With each tiny root, it pushed through the air.

As leaves unfurl with a sassy twirl,
It giggles at clouds that swirl and whirl.
'Look at me soaring, I'm part of the scene,
A splash of green joy, bright and serene!'

## Whispered Secrets of Soil and Sun

In the darkness, whispers start to bloom,
Secrets exchanged in the earthen room.
'What's it like up there?' the seedlet sighed,
'Under the blue skies, where all dreams glide?'

The soil chuckled, 'Patience, dear sprite,
Soon you'll be dancing in broad daylight.'
With sunlight streaming, it felt so bold,
'Time to emerge, let the magic unfold!'

A shake of its roots and it poked out its head,
'There's far more to life than just this bed!'
With laughter and joy, it stretched to the sun,
And whispered back, 'Oh boy, this is fun!'

## Seeds of Change in a Global Garden

In a garden far and wide,
Seeds gather, side by side.
Each one claims, 'I'm the best!'
With a leafy little jest.

One says, 'I'll be a tree!'
Another laughs, 'No, just a pea!'
In this bickering, they sway,
Dreaming big, in green array.

Worms debate with bugs in tow,
On who makes the soil glow.
'I've a worm's-eye view!' they boast,
While the compost's yeast makes toast.

Under sunshine, all unite,
Chasing shadows, bath in light.
Life blooms with a silly twist,
In this garden, none are missed.

## Child's Play in a Plant's Sanctuary

Tiny hands scoop and dig,
Amid the sprouts, all so big.
Laughing at the muddy splats,
Who needs toys when there are hats?

Crafty leaves become a crown,
Worn by kings of upsidedown.
Dressed in garment made of green,
Royalty in dirt, a scene!

Giggling daisies, bright and bold,
Tell the stories yet untold.
Jumping beans dance in a row,
Making music, don't you know?

Games of catch with flying seeds,
Whispers shared among the weeds.
In this fun, the plants all cheer,
For the children, we hold dear.

## Living Portraits of Nature's Devotion

In pots where colors blend,
Natural wonders twist and bend.
Petals pose like models grand,
In a photo stop, oh so planned.

Succulents pout, cacti smile,
For a selfie, they'll wait a while.
'Look at us with all our charms!'
Nature's ticking, lush alarms!

Fungus paints in shades of gray,
Over shadows, come what may.
Mold and moss join in the fun,
Nature's canvas, never done.

Snap a shot, preserve the grace,
In this pot, we set the pace.
Living portraits, shifts and sways,
In this odd, delightful craze.

## The Quiet Chronicles of Sprouting Life

In silence, seeds begin to scheme,
Hatching plans, a verdant dream.
'What if I grew taller fast?'
With roots that hold, a sturdy cast.

Little sprouts with voices low,
Murmur tales of rain and glow.
'Tomorrow's sun will bring us cheer!'
In whispers, dreams appear.

Their dreams unfold, a leafy lore,
While dodging shadows evermore.
Each sprout a tale of joy or woe,
In this pot, their stories flow.

With patience, they reach for the sky,
Determined sprouts that never sigh.
Chronicles of growth abide,
In this quiet, joyful ride.

## **Boundless Potential in a Terracotta Home**

In a clay container, dreams can sprout,
Cabbage wears a tutu, dancing about.
Radishes giggle, with hats on their heads,
While beans tell jokes from their leafy beds.

Sunshine strokes soil, with giggles and grace,
Worms hold a concert, a wormy embrace.
Beetroot's a joker, with roots deep in the ground,
In this happy pot, no frowns to be found.

## **Reflections of a Gardener's Heart**

Sprouts in the morning, oh what a sight,
Peas make a pyramid, quite a delight.
Broccoli boasts of its green, sturdy flair,
Carrots in tuxedos, preparing to share.

Sunflower pokes its head, playful and tall,
Says, 'I've heard of the gala, now who's got the ball?'
Tomatoes are blushing, ripe with delight,
In this pot party, all's merry and bright!

## Life's Canvas in Bound Earth

In colors of green, a masterpiece blooms,
Petunias chatter in vibrant costumes.
Hyacinths laugh, they put on a show,
While thyme makes puns about 'thyme for a grow!'

Pansies gossip in shades of pure cheer,
'Who wore it best?' they giggle and leer.
Succulents striking the latest cool pose,
In this earthen gallery, happiness grows.

## Moments Captured in a Sunlit Vessel

Sunlight fills this bustling tiny home,
Chives in the corner pretending to roam.
Basil cracks jokes, laughing with zest,
Mint rolls its eyes, "I'm clearly the best!"

A fairy-tale scene among roots and bloom,
As veggies hold court, dispelling the gloom.
With laughter and cheer, they unite in their plot,
In their sunny abode, happiness is caught.

## Sheltered by the Sky

A cactus in a window, oh what a sight,
With arms raised high, it greets the light.
Proudly perched on a tiny chair,
Its spiky demeanor gives folks a scare.

Watering day arrives, what a fun task,
A gentle sprinkle, is that too much to ask?
I trip and spill, oh heavens, no!
The plant smiles wide, as if in a show.

## Tendrils of Hope

Little sprout peeking, with a green little head,
Wonders if it's true, the stories I said.
"Grow tall and free, just reach for the stars!"
A hopeful whisper from tiny avatars.

A snail wanders by, really quite slow,
"Hey, what's the rush?  I'm not here to glow!"
With humor they share, in an earthy embrace,
A garden of giggles, in this vibrant place.

## The Art of Nurturing

My plants demand love, oh what a high toll,
"Feed us with care, or lose your soul!"
With fertilizers mixed, it's a painter's delight,
Each leaf a canvas, green and bright.

Pruning is art, at least that's the claim,
But I snip off a petal and play the blame game.
"Who knew your haircuts would bring such despair?"
A house full of plants causes quite the affair!

## **Thrum of Life in Stillness**

In a corner they sway, my leafy brigade,
Marching in silence, quite the charade.
They whisper and rustle, with mischief at heart,
Challenging me to figure their art.

A spider spins webs, with dreams of its own,
"Hey! I'm just here to mooch, not to be shown!"
With laughter they jive, in a pot there's a dance,
Life's quirky moments, oh what a chance!

## Cradled in Clay

A mug of clay, so stout and round,
Holds secrets whispered, laughter found.
With every sip, a joke takes flight,
In tepid tea or coffee bright.

Dancing crumbs from cookies' reign,
One splash of milk, they squawk in vain.
Oh, what a sight, the spill is grand,
Cup-sized chaos at my hand!

Stirring spoons that chime like bells,
Each clink a tale that it tells.
In quiet corners, mess abounds,
Raise your cup for joy that sounds!

Cradled snug, amidst the fray,
Oh, what fun this pot can play!
When life gets tough, just take a break,
And watch your teacup laugh and shake!

## Flourish Under the Hearth

Nestled warm, beneath the glow,
Sprouting herbs, they dance and grow.
Thyme's got sass, and basil's bold,
They gossip sweetly, stories told.

Chives, they whisper, oh-so-sly,
With garlicky dreams, they never shy.
In cozy pots, they plot and scheme,
Awaiting dinner's tasty dream.

Potted plants and kitchen jams,
Roasted veggies, merry clams.
With each delight, they have their say,
Cooking up fun in a playful way!

When guests arrive, it's quite the show,
A floral feast, with antics to throw.
Underneath the hearth's warm heart,
The joy of food is just the start!

# The Dance of Petals

In vibrant pots, the petals sway,
Touching sunlight, come what may.
Daisies giggle, roses spin,
In pollen parties, they always win!

Fluttering leaves, a bustling crew,
Sipping raindrops, what a view!
They toss their colors, bold and loud,
Shouting praises, feeling proud.

Caterpillars slide down the stems,
In the garden's wild, little gems.
Every blossom, a laughing face,
Life's a dance, with flow and grace.

So grow your pot, let joy unfurl,
In this tiny world, watch them twirl.
Each bloom a joke, each leaf a friend,
In clumsy steps that never end!

## Hidden Stories of the Heart

Within each pot, tales remain,
Where laughter lingers, joy sustains.
Geraniums hum a happy tune,
Whispering secrets beneath the moon.

Peppers jive, and radishes sing,
A spicy salsa in the spring.
While beans throw shade, quite unashamed,
In garden games, they're never tamed.

Soil's the stage for comedic quests,
Where plants perform their leafy tests.
Every sprout a risky chance,
In nature's blooms, they love to prance.

With pots of cheer, hearts light and free,
In every sprout, a legacy.
So laugh along with every plant,
For in their growth, there's much to chant!

## Fragmented Life in a Whimsical Vessel

In a bowl so round, where chaos resides,
A cactus insists it can fit with the fries.
A fern dreams of oceans, but water is rare,
While daisies debate who has the best hair.

The thyme likes to gossip with basil so spry,
While mint starts a rumor that parsley can fly.
The pot's a grand stage, where blooms laugh and sway,
A circus of greens in the sun's bright display.

Oh, what a ruckus, this leafy brigade,
Each stem has a story, each shade is afraid.
They thrive in their folly, in soil they confide,
A quirky assembly, with nature as guide.

So if you should visit this home full of cheer,
Remember to chuckle at all you hold dear.
For life can be silly, just look at this show,
A vibrant parade in a world made of dough.

## Artistry of Nature in a Cultured Home

A lettuce wears glasses, quite chic and refined,
While parsley's a painter, all colors combined.
A pot serves as canvas, where dreams bloom and spark,
With talents galore, they like to leave their mark.

A radish recites poetry, rhymes all the rage,
While carrots narrate tales from their humble page.
The soil serves as gallery, rich with their art,
A masterpiece lives in each leafy little heart.

Tomatoes strut proudly, a bit plump and red,
While bell peppers murmur, 'We've got it instead!'
A veggie soirée, with costumes so bright,
Each dressed in their foliage, what a delight!

In this cultured enclave, where plants call the shots,
Who knew home could house such illustrious thoughts?
So come for a visit, there's plenty to see,
Where nature's art school runs wild and free!

## The Delicate Balance of Green and Clay

In a pot of wild wonders, a peace treaty brews,
Where succulents gossip about yesterday's snooze.
The dirt's always shifting, a comical dance,
As roots form new friendships, and stems take a chance.

The chives, always sharp, make the garlic all pout,
While sage plays the wise one, occasionally loud.
A crouton of cosmos does cartwheels, how fun,
In a garden of giggles, they bask in the sun.

With water for laughter and sunlight for cheer,
The petals conspire, "Let's make our pot clear!"
They stretch and they twiddle, a plant fiesta craze,
A jolly ensemble wrapped up in green ways.

So tiptoe on in, this pot's quite the sight,
In nature's grand circus, all's merry and bright.
A quirky collection, your spirit will lift,
Among leafy companions, you'll find quite a gift.

## Cozy Cradle of Flora and Dreams

In a cradle of green, where fancies take flight,
A sprout dreams of rainbows, all colors so bright.
The soil is a pillow, so comfy and deep,
Each seed holds a secret, a commit to keep.

The daisies throw parties and giggle at dusk,
While violets plot pranks in their velvety husk.
A houseplant with style, a diva so grand,
Winks at the others, 'Just follow my brand.'

The geraniums gossip, a scandalous lot,
While ferns fan their fronds like, 'What have you got?'
The pot is their palace, a whimsical place,
Where dreams are the guest and laughter keeps pace.

So come take a peek at this cozy abode,
Where flora and fables reside on this road.
A whimsical haven where fun never dims,
The joy of creation bursts forth from its whims.

## Moments in Green Guarded By Glass

In a corner, they sit in splendor,
Beans and peas in small containers.
Waving leaves like tiny flags,
Chasing sunlight without banter.

A radish jokes, 'I'm quite a root!'
While garlic whispers, 'Hey, what's the loot?'
Each sprout giggles, 'I must confess,
I'm still not sure what's of more use.'

They dream of clouds, of rain so sweet,
Telling tales of sunny heat.
A berry blushes, quite the tease,
'Wait till I'm ripe, you'll want a treat!'

And when the door swings open wide,
They plot their escape, excitement's tide.
But stuck inside, they'll sing and cheer,
In glassy homes, their joys abide.

## Roots Tangle

In shadows deep where roots entwine,
A carrot nudges, 'This space is mine!'
Beets are laughing, 'Let's take a chance,
Join the twisty, wiggle dance!'

Potatoes grumble, 'Give me some room!'
While onions plot a sneaky bloom.
They dig and tease, a messy game,
'Tangled together, we'll find our fame!'

Squash rolls over, 'Hey, what's the fuss?'
'Can't we all share in this big ol' bus?'
Roots laugh deep, they know the score,
In this tight space, they'd all explore.

Thus they grow, so close, so tight,
In twists and turns, they bloom in light.
With laughter sprouting where they unite,
Together they journey, what a delight!

**Dreams Unfold**

In a pot where visions rise,
A flower dreams of sunny skies.
'Will I dance in a garden fair?'
Pondering petals in gentle care.

Her neighbor, a sprout, nods in glee,
'One day we'll sway as wild and free!'
With giggles shared like crinkled leaves,
Their hopes hang high; believe, believe!

Basil and sage weave tales of spice,
With mossy whispers, oh so nice.
They twirl and sprinkle magic dust,
In this bloom, they happily trust.

Yet when the rain comes pouring down,
They huddle close, no need to frown.
Each drop brings life, each moment bold,
As laughter blooms and dreams unfold!

## A World Within the Walls

Inside a pot, a realm is spun,
Where tiny critters join the fun.
A ladybug's a queen on a leaf,
Hosting parties, causing belief!

Frogs in clay say, 'Let's play a game!'
While worms squirm, never feeling lame.
With laughter bubbling like morning dew,
They cheer on sprouts in splendid hue.

A knock on glass brings curious eyes,
'What's going on behind those skies?'
They wave their leaves, the hidden crowd,
'Join the laughter; we're all so loud!'

From tiny seeds to vines that leap,
Within these walls, their secrets keep.
In a world so small, such joy we find,
With every sprout, their hearts entwined.

## Harmony in a Humble Vessel

In humble soil where laughter leans,
Each sprout giggles at silly scenes.
Tomatoes blushing, 'Look at me!'
While herbs shout tunes, 'We're wild and free!'

A humble pot, yet filled with cheer,
As roots embrace, they persevere.
They trade their jokes and tasty plans,
Cooking dreams with tiny hands.

Chives tell tales of days gone past,
As radishes reply, 'Life goes so fast!'
With every spritz of morning air,
They twirl and whirl without a care.

So raise a glass to this merry crew,
In a gentle pot, they start anew.
With harmony sweet in their little space,
There's magic found in every trace!

## Cozy Corners of Growth and Serenity

In a corner where the sunlight plays,
A tiny sprout has found its ways.
Dancing leaves in green and gold,
Whispers of tales waiting to be told.

A sock that's lost, a shoe askew,
In this snug space, they seem to brew.
Mix them all, and what do you see?
A jungle of wonders, just for me!

The pots giggle as roots intertwine,
They share secrets over sips of brine.
Dirt beneath nails, a joyful spree,
Sprouting laughter as wild as can be.

Oh little plants, with mischief in tow,
In muddy puddles, you put on a show.
With each new leaf, a cheer goes out,
In this cozy spot, there's always clout.

## The Enchantment of Pot-Preserved Potential

Nestled snug in a ceramic crown,
Peeking out, never feeling down.
With swirls of paint and charming hues,
Each pot holds magic, in life's sweet cues.

Water lightly, let laughter bloom,
Tiny wonders call for more room.
Not just a home, but a laughter spree,
As roots wiggle in peculiar glee.

When friends drop by, pots take a bow,
With tales of growth upon the brow.
Exchanging puns with petunias near,
A whimsical dance, that's oh so dear.

Every drop of soil tells a tale,
Of adventures lived without fail.
In these vessels, humor finds its way,
In pots of joy, we all want to stay.

## Shadows and Light in Clay's Embrace

In clay they dwell, both shy and bold,
A spectacle of stories to be told.
Shadows hug the plants so tight,
While sunbeams wrestle them with light.

Each clip and snip makes quite the mess,
A garden party in floral dress.
Smiling daisies chat with thyme,
As laughter echoes, weaving rhyme.

Overhead, the old ceiling fan,
Winks at the chaos, plots a plan.
In this pot, a circus thrives,
With leafy acrobats, the fun derives.

They sway and dance in the afternoon,
In their clay home, they feel immune.
With roots in soil and dreams afloat,
In light and shadow, they daily gloat.

## Confinement of Dreams in a Scented Haven

In a pot, where whimsy lies,
A patch of dreams and tiny sighs.
Mint and basil play hide and seek,
In this aromatic nook, they peek.

Each sprout and leaf, a silly scheme,
Growing upward toward the dream.
Caught up in fragrance, they chuckle aloud,
Amongst the herbs, they form a crowd.

When winds of change begin to blow,
The pots will wobble, stealing the show.
With every shake, the soil confesses,
These green delights hold funny guesses.

While humans hover with watering can,
The plants perform their wild, odd plan.
In this scented bastion, joy's a song,
In quirky pots, we all belong.

## A Journey Beneath Fragile Leaves

In a world of dirt and dream,
Tiny critters plot and scheme.
A pot, their ship, a leafy sail,
Adventures grow with each detail.

Worms throw parties, roots join in,
Sipping dew as it begins.
Ladybugs dance on the rim,
While cacti shake it, looking grim.

Sunlight tickles, shadows sway,
Banana peels spill in play.
Potato plans a heist tonight,
But lettuce keeps it all in sight.

Oh, what fun, this leafy crew,
With secrets shared in morning dew.
Each sprout a friend, each twig a jest,
Beneath the leaves, they love their quest.

## Time's Dance in a Botanical Sphere


Tick-tock goes the watering can,
In a twist, a daisy ran.
Salsa moves on soil so fine,
As thyme and basil sip their wine.

Snails arrive in fancy hats,
Throwing shade at jumpy brats.
Pansies giggle, tulips blush,
In that garden, there's no rush.

The sun climbs high, the shadows stretch,
A pot's a stage, no need to sketch.
Funky fronds prance in delight,
Bending low, no fear of height.

Here, the laughter never ends,
Each leaf a joke; they are best friends.
Time waltzes with each playful bloom,
Within this sphere, there's always room.

## Roots Reaching for Tomorrow's Light

Roots are tangled, growing wide,
In their dance, they often hide.
Reaching up for dreams so bright,
In the dark, they plot at night.

Potatoes whisper, tales untold,
With carrots boasting, brave and bold.
A rebel radish, sensing fate,
While thyme predicts a crazy date.

Underneath, the soil's chat,
A secret club of spade and hat.
Ginger jokes with every sprout,
While petty weeds just pout and shout.

Each tickle from the garden's crust,
Ignites their laughter and their trust.
Tomorrow's light is on its way,
In every root, their hopes will stay.

## Rain's Breath in a Small Container

Pitter-patter, drops arrive,
In the pot, they jump and dive.
Raindrops giggle, puddles form,
Creating magic in the storm.

Lettuce sings a soggy tune,
While peas throw darts; oh, what a boon!
Cacti frown, but soon they grin,
Singing praises for this win.

Basil's dancing, herbs align,
In the rain, they intertwine.
Their leaf parade, a flouncy sight,
With humor in each splash of light.

Oh, what joy this weather brings,
In every drop, a pot that sings.
With every sniff of rain's pure zest,
In this container, plants are blessed.

## Enclosed Beauty in Adaptive Existence

A cactus dreams of being a tree,
Yet in its pot, it's quite carefree.
It stretches wide, with all its might,
Thinking it's the star of the night.

A herb hums tunes from the kitchen's side,
While a fern looks on, full of pride.
They gossip sweetly about the sun,
While plotting how to have more fun.

A little pea jumps up with glee,
"I'm not just dinner, I'm fancy!"
It wears a leaf like a crown so bright,
Declaring, "I'm the royal delight!"

The pot's a stage, the roots take flight,
Dancing below, hidden from sight.
With laughter sprinkled in every sprout,
Who knew being small could be such a rout?

## Tranquil Harmonies Beneath Leafy Expressions

In a small space where sunlight weaves,
Plants hum their tunes, caught on leaves.
A basil whispers secrets to thyme,
While each pot winks, feeling sublime.

A tiny sunflower tries to spin,
But ends up waving a bit too thin.
"Look at me!" it shouts with glee,
"I'm a giant! Can't you see?"

Lettuce lounges, feeling so cool,
While mint teases, "You're quite the fool!"
But lettuce just chuckles, unfazed by the jest,
"I'm crunchy and fresh—who's really the best?"

A peace lily leans, sophisticated and wise,
Sipping on droplets, it sighs with surprise.
"What a party we have in this booth,
With every green friend, we tell the truth!"

## The Echo of Life in a Miniature World


Tiny beans chatter about their dreams,
While brussels sprouts burst at the seams.
"I'm meant to become a gourmet feast!"
Squeaks one sprout, feeling quite pleased.

Within these confines, a drama unfolds,
Potatoes plot as their tale is told.
"We'll escape some day, rise from this fate!"
While carrots giggle, cringing at fate.

The air is thick with friendly banter,
As radishes play their tiny canter.
"Let's plan a heist, let's break this pot!
Or shall we stay, be cozy, not caught?"

Basil nods, "Oh what a sight!
Let's stay a bit more, it feels so right!"
In laughter, they find their fate entwined,
In pots of dreams, where joy is defined.

## Sacred Breath in a Nurturing Chamber

In a chamber small, a fern brightens day,
With a sassy twist, it sways and plays.
"A leaf can dance! Look at my flair!"
It teases, with no signs of care.

A plucky mint, with scents so bold,
Claims the title of king—unfold!
While thyme just rolls, amused and light,
"You're king of what? A pot, alright!"

In a sunny nook, a story spins,
With seedlings grinning, where life begins.
"Let's write a script, we'll be the stars!
Pot actors in comedies, showing off scars!"

As raindrops gurgle and laughter spills,
Each little plant gives winter chills.
In this merry realm, small wonders birth,
In the sacred joy of a leafy hearth.

## Salt and Soil: The Rooted Experience

In a realm of grit and fluff,
Seeds dance in the earth, oh so tough.
Worms wiggle with glee below,
While sprouts peek out, putting on a show.

Water splashes, oh what a splash,
Plants in pots grow with panache.
Sunshine beams, the leaves all cheer,
Roots whisper secrets, loud and clear.

Who knew dirt could be so grand?
With every sprout, we make our stand.
A tangle of greens, a rainbow in sight,
In pots we trust, our small green delight.

So here we toil, with light hearts and spade,
Giggling as we sow the trade.
Life's silliness in every sprout,
Salt and soil, what life's about!

## Jewel of Growth in Containers of Care

A pot of wonders, a treasure chest,
With little green jewels, we feel so blessed.
Buds popping out like confetti in June,
Each leaf a laugh, all singing a tune.

Tiny gardeners with dreams in hand,
Digging right in, oh isn't it grand?
With watering cans, we march like a band,
Growing our laughter, just as we planned.

Roses may wilt, but smiles will last,
Planting our hopes, we're free and fast.
A pot full of joy, who could resist?
In this garden, life is pure bliss!

So here's to the blooms, both big and small,
In our pot kingdom, we thrive through it all.
With dirt on our hands and joy on our face,
In a world of green, we've found our place!

## Pottery of Life's Many Colors

In pots like palettes, colors collide,
Bright yellows and reds, with nowhere to hide.
Each plant a painter, a stroke so bold,
Together they giggle, and never grow old.

Mix and match, in a playful dance,
Leaves are laughing, they love the chance.
Petals twirl in the warm, soft light,
Creating a scene, such a joyful sight!

The clay holds stories, both wild and sweet,
Life's funny quirks grow under our feet.
In every sprout, a family's tale,
As we nourish dreams without fail.

So let's grab our pots, and paint the way,
With laughter and love, we'll brighten our day.
A medley of shades, together we blend,
In this art of growth, the humor won't end!

## **Fragrant Beginnings within Clay Walls**

In clay walls we dream, with scents in the air,
A basil bouquet, oh who could compare?
Mint teasing the nose, such a friendly face,
In this little garden, we find our space.

Chatter of roots, like gossiping friends,
Reminding us all, life happily bends.
With a sniff of rosemary, we chuckle and cheer,
Every herb tells a tale, bringing smiles near.

A pot of perfume, a feast for the soul,
With laughter and joy, it's our ultimate goal.
So here in our pots, the humor's no ruse,
Each fragrant beginning, we gladly choose!

Let's water our dreams, let light embrace,
In our quirky garden, we take our place.
With each new sprout, fresh jokes we'll unfurl,
In fragrant beginnings, we've found our world!

## The Symphony of Green and Growth

In a sunny corner, things start to sprout,
A leafy orchestra, without a doubt.
Tiny trumpets of green sing with glee,
Roots dance below, as wild as can be.

Watering can, conductor of this show,
Plants waving hands, putting on a glow.
Pots snug and cozy, a plant party bold,
With their leafy antics, stories unfold.

Dancing daisies on a tabletop stage,
While snappy succulents act their age.
A bromeliad twirls, a quirky affair,
Nature's own jesters, without a care.

From seedlings to giants, they just can't wait,
To join the fun at the garden gate.
Life's little circus, in pots, it's grand,
In this verdant world, laughter is planned.

## Oasis of Wonder on the Windowsill

Sunshine brightens this little zone,
Each plant a friend, never alone.
Cacti are jokers with spiky attire,
While ferns in the breeze seem to conspire.

Herbs whisper secrets of dinner delight,
While succulents smirk in the soft twilight.
A basil leaf winks, a thyme starts to hum,
This windowsill party is just so much fun!

Kale's doing calisthenics over there,
While mint and chives show off their flair.
Together they giggle in pots side by side,
In this ecosystem, laughter can't hide.

Night falls gently, the day comes to rest,
But their bedtime antics are nothing but zest.
In this oasis, the smiles never fade,
A world of whimsy in a glass cascade.

## Petals of Promise Under Glass

Behind the glass, a world wakes anew,
With petals and colors, every shade a clue.
Buds popping open, a party inside,
Whispering secrets they giggle and slide.

Tiny drummers beat on pots so round,
While blooms burst forth, in laughter they're bound.
Dahlias compete for the crown of the day,
In this floral fun, they frolic and play.

Leaves strut their stuff, with vibrant displays,
In this glassy abode, chaos obeys.
Jars filled with soil and quirky delight,
Bring cheer to the morn and a twinkle at night.

With roots interlaced, they sing soft and low,
In this petal parade, the good vibes flow.
In jars of glass, their joy never stops,
For laughter is endless in their little shops.

## **Echoes of Nature in a Tiny Space**

In a nook where the sunlight dances bright,
Petunias chuckle at the morning light.
Tiny terracotta houses lined in a row,
Beneath every leaf, a whimsical show.

Tiny tomatoes with their mischievous gleam,
Whispering stories from a garden dream.
Potting soil giggles when touched with a hand,
Creating new mischief with every grain of sand.

Orchids toss petals, a confetti affair,
While a garden gnome grins with a cheeky stare.
In laughter and green, they spread such delight,
Each plant a performer, at the edge of night.

Sharing their tales in a soft, gentle hum,
In this tiny universe, life's never dumb.
Echoes of nature in every little seam,
In the concert of green, they live out their dream.

## **Stars Within a Bound Space**

In a bowl, a universe glows,
A carrot dreams and a pea doze.
The tomato spins tales of light,
While herbs gossip in whispers, just right.

Basil puts on a leafy show,
While beans stretch high, to steal the glow.
The pot becomes a stage for play,
With veggies dancing, come what may.

A sprinkle of salt, a dash of flair,
Garlic jokes float up in the air.
Potatoes ponder life's big plan,
While onions roll and laugh — oh man!

In this small realm, a great surprise,
Where laughter simmers and joy can rise.
Every meal served, a grand delight,
Together we feast, what a funny sight!

## Nature's Tapestry in Tiny Realms

In a cup, a garden thrives,
Tiny creatures, joy arrives.
A snail zooms on a leaf's green glide,
As peas and sprouts play peek and hide.

A ladybug wears a dapper hat,
While beans sway as if in chat.
The pot's a circus of green delight,
Where sprouts have dreams that soar to new heights.

Radishes gossip about the sun,
And all agree that life's just fun.
Their roots dig deep, while leaves cheer wide,
"Life's a party!" They sing with pride.

In this world of small surprise,
Where every veggie winks its eyes.
Morning glories laugh with glee,
Nature's tapestry, pure comedy!

## **Nightfall Among the Leaves**

Underneath a moon so bright,
Leaves whisper tales of pure delight.
A cucumber winks, steals the show,
While cherry tomatoes are all aglow.

Onions sigh and share their dreams,
While broccoli bursts at the seams.
"What's cooking?" asks a sprightly sprout,
As shadows dance, there's laughter about.

The night's alive with veggie schemes,
Carrots plot secret little dreams.
Beet greens twirl in a twinkling dance,
In this pot, they live to prance.

Stars peek in, trying to see,
What fun awaits the jolly pea.
In the hush of night, oh what a scene,
A veggie party, lively and keen!

# Reawakening in the Morning Light

With dawn comes laughter, a morning tune,
  Each plant stretches to greet the noon.
  Herbs shake off their dreamy sleeps,
    As sunlight tickles, the pot leaps.

Radishes laugh, chasing shadows away,
    While peas giggle, ready to play.
    Excited sprouts hop in delight,
  "Let's fill our days, oh what a sight!"

Carrots tosses out a sun-baked wish,
  A scallion twirls, "Where's my dish?"
  The pot fills up with warm sunlight,
As laughter bubbles — such pure delight!

In every leaf, the joy unfolds,
  A tale of morning, bright and bold.
  The pot awakens, it knows its role,
To bring forth happiness from the soul!

## Immured Beauty with Roots of Resilience

In a tiny home, plants thrive,
With roots that dance and leaves that jive.
A cactus wearing a sombrero,
Sips morning sun and sings like a hero.

A fern with curls, so full of flair,
Winks at the window, catching the air.
A mischievous herb, green and spry,
Dreams of adventures, oh my, oh my!

Peeking through soil, they plot and play,
While humans rush through another day.
In their little world, laughter's a must,
With every sprout, they build up trust.

So here's to the green, the silly, the bright,
In their colorful pots, they bask in delight.
With roots so deep and humor so vast,
These little ones teach us to laugh and last.

## The Gracious Giver of Nurtured Greens

With every sprinkle of water, life is stirred,
A little basil speaks, but is often unheard.
It dreams of pasta, so savory and bold,
While seeking sunbeams, perfect and gold.

The cilantro giggles, its aroma a tease,
As thyme tells tales of honeyed bees.
Each leaf has a story, each stem has a grin,
In this verdant place, the laughter begins.

They share their wisdom, oh so sprightly,
Advising on kindness and living rightly.
A kaleidoscope of green, so vibrant and bright,
They dance in their pots, a hilarious sight.

So thank the greens, unique and spry,
For offering smiles, they sure can amplify.
In tiny spaces, their jests resonate,
Reminding us all - joy doesn't wait!

## Tales Intertwined with Vines and Roots

In the corner, a vine climbs high,
Whispering secrets as it reaches the sky.
It tickles the curtains, flutters like lace,
Creating a world of friendly embrace.

A tomato plant boasts of fruits so red,
While a cheeky pepper dreams of being fed.
They share late-night giggles, stories so grand,
Of daring adventures in this little land.

Across the shelf, a patch of mint,
Jokes about flavors that make us squint.
With every burst, it charms and confounds,
Turning dull meals to joyful rounds.

So gather around, all loves of green,
For the tales we weave are a hearty scene.
In pots and planters, their joys arise,
In laughter's embrace, beneath friendly skies.

## Moments of Joy Amidst the Foliage

A rubber plant's stance is a royal decree,
While a pothos twirls like a dancer, carefree.
They bask in the spotlight, drama unfolds,
As fun little stories in greenlight they hold.

The air plants laugh with a cheeky flair,
Hanging around, they just don't care.
While the lanai garden throws a wild tea,
Each leaf a character, joyfully free.

A garden gnome chuckles, with a wink and a grin,
As herbs in a row have a show, let's begin!
With thyme and dill hosting comedy night,
The audience plants giggle at every delight.

So let's raise our glasses to green friends we know,
In pots so tiny, their spirits do grow.
With humor and heart in rich soil and cheer,
They teach us to laugh, year after year.

## Secrets Shared in Chlorophyll's Shade

In the garden, whispers fly,
The lettuce grins, the beans all sigh.
Tomatoes dance, in their viney dress,
While carrots giggle, feeling quite blessed.

The radishes play hide and seek,
Beneath the leaves, they laugh and peek.
Herbs tell tales of flavors bold,
While beans recount stories of days of old.

The zucchini flaunts its yellow streak,
Claiming it's the best, so sleek and chic.
Cucumbers wonder, 'Am I a snack?'
As sunflowers nod, with smiles they lack.

Each leaf a secret, each sprout a jest,
In this green world, we are truly blessed.
With roots and shoots, together we thrive,
In this shady realm, we come alive.

## Peeking into Potpourri's Hidden Worlds

A jellybean pot sits on the shelf,
Thinking it's the chef of its own self.
Fragrant whispers from flowers galore,
Promising a scent to make you explore.

Lavender lounges, wearing a crown,
Rosemary rules with a floral frown.
Mint giggles, fresh and spry,
While cinnamon stretches, reaching for the sky.

A sneaky dried orange slips off the plate,
Chasing a rogue clove—it's quite the fate!
Nutmeg chuckles, blending in the mess,
As thyme takes notes, learning from the rest.

In this potpourri, all scents can play,
Each sprinkle of spice brings joy to the day.
With laughter and fragrance woven so tight,
These hidden worlds bring pure delight.

## Emblems of Renewal on Sunny Days

Sunshine spills on a painted pot,
Where daisies wink, and everything's hot.
Basil's green head is held proudly high,
While marigolds flirt, waving hello shy.

A sunflower spins, with seeds in tow,
Boasting its height, putting on a show.
Petunias gossip, their blooms so bright,
Each petal a story, a colorful sight.

As bees orchestrate a buzzing dance,
In their sweet world, they take a chance.
Ladybugs prance on a leaf's ballet,
Emblems of joy on a sunlit day.

With nature's art, this scene unfolds,
Funny little moments that life upholds.
In pots of laughter, sunshine they know,
A garden of giggles, putting on a show.

## Small Wonders on a Playful Patch

In a tiny patch, the fun begins,
With a chorus of veggies, they all spin.
Radishes twirl, bright red and round,
While little peas giggle, all snug and sound.

A playful potato hides in the dirt,
Wishing for adventures, a little exert.
Corn leans in close, sharing a grin,
Telling tales of the winds and the spin.

Tiny sprouts peek from the earth so deep,
Dreaming of mornings when they'll leap.
Zucchini jokes about its long, green fate,
While bell peppers plot, you might call it fate.

In this playful patch, laughter's a must,
Where each little plant sparks joy and trust.
Together they grow, with silliness rife,
In this little world, that's the wonder of life.

## Portraits of Flavor and Fragrance

In a cozy nook where veggies dance,
Tomatoes blush, while radishes prance.
Basil's whispers mix with thyme,
As garlic sighs, 'Oh, isn't this sublime?'

Onions giggle, they bring the zest,
Carrots chuckle, feeling their best.
Peas in pods just can't hold tight,
They burst with laughter, what a sight!

Cabbage rolls with a leafy flair,
Zucchini jokes land without a care.
Each flavor's portrait, vibrant and bright,
Gathering for a culinary night!

So raise a toast to this funny crew,
In pots and pans, they form a brew.
With every stir and every twirl,
The kitchen's filled with laughter's whirl.

## **Beyond the Surface: Growth's Secret**

Beneath the soil, a tickle compiles,
Seeds whisper secrets with mischievous smiles.
Worms wiggle by, giving a nod,
'We've got the dirt, wait till they applaud!'

Sprouts peek out with a cheeky grin,
'We're ready for sunshine, let the fun begin!'
Roots burrow deep for a chuckle or two,
While sipping on dew from a morning brew.

"Plant me, water me, toss in some cheer!"
Said the little lettuce with no hint of fear.
Life underground is a party so grand,
With all of them plotting to take a stand!

So as they rise, let's all rejoice,
In this garden's dance, they've found their voice.
Oh, what a revel, the pot's full of glee,
Sprouting their magic for all to see!

## When Seasons Embrace

Springtime giggles, blooms in a whirl,
Bees buzzing round in a happy swirl.
Carrots pop out, looking so bright,
"With every season, we'll keep it light!"

Summer sizzles, bringing the fun,
Tomatoes wink under the hot sun.
Chillies shout, 'Spice it up, my friend!'
As they revel, they'll never end.

Autumn chuckles with pumpkins galore,
'Let's bake some goods or maybe more!'
Squash joins in, inventing a dish,
With all this laughter, who needs a wish?

Winter whispers, softening the cheer,
Soup pots bubble, warm up your ear.
'Time for comfort, let's cozy up tight!'
In this pot of seasons, laughter's so bright.

## **Serenity in a Simple Circle**

In a circular pot, they gather and play,
Every veggie has something funny to say.
Radishes join in with a tap-tap rhymes,
Creating a melody, oh, such fun times!

Peppers and onions, in a colorful mix,
Share stories about their culinary tricks.
Garlic chimes in, 'I've got the class,
A hint of me and things will amass!'

Spinach shouts, 'I'm the leafy queen!'
While herbs laugh about where they've all been.
This pot of joy, a comedy scene,
Mixing the flavors, rich and serene.

So here's to the circle, this wacky crew,
Potluck of laughter, we bid adieu.
In every dish, there's a sprinkle of fun,
Together they flourish, each and every one!

## Whispers Among the Roots

In the dark, they shuffle and sway,
Tiny voices chatter away.
Worms tell tales of dirt and grime,
While old roots gossip, feeling fine.

A bean sprout dreams of being tall,
But fears the wind might make it fall.
Leaves laugh loudly at sundry woes,
As bugs parade in funny clothes.

Water droplets waltz in glee,
Tickling roots like a ticklish bee.
Fungi dance, wearing caps so bright,
In a rhizome rave, a silly sight!

In this pot, all jesters meet,
Making friends with every beet.
With each sprout come quirky tales,
Their joy erupts! It never pales.

## Brewed Dreams in Silence

In a teapot, dreams take flight,
Steeping thoughts through day and night.
Herbs and spices, a fragrant mess,
Counting bubbles, no need to stress.

A slice of lemon, a dash of fun,
Mischiefs brewed beneath the sun.
Giggles rise with the steaming tea,
A drop of honey for glee, you see!

But watch out for the sneaky spoon,
It stirs up laughter, morning to noon.
A dance that spills and spills again,
Causing chuckles in the drain.

So sip your tea, let worries fade,
In this pot, no plans are made.
Just brewing joy, sweet and calm,
Every sip holds a little charm.

## Growth Beneath the Surface

Down below, the party ignites,
Roots entwined in silly fights.
A carrot juggles dirt with glee,
While radishes boast, "Look at me!"

Underneath, the rhizomes twirl,
With each twist, a hidden pearl.
Carbs in costumes make quite the scene,
Turning soil into a dance routine.

Potatoes in shades of brown and blue,
Whisper jokes just for the crew.
They pop up, but they just can't quit,
Beneath the layers, they still commit!

They tumble with laughter, a riotous spread,
In the compost, where dreams are fed.
Where roots become the stars of the play,
And silly antics make the day.

## Fragile Greens in Sunlight

Delicate leaves in the sun do prance,
Basking in light, they take a chance.
They rustle and flutter, a leafy cheer,
Sharing secrets that only they hear.

A gentle breeze picks up their song,
They sway to the rhythm, all day long.
Tiny ants join the dappled dance,
In this garden of green, all take a chance.

The basil blushes, the lettuce grins,
Join the giggles as the fun begins.
With every petal that twirls in grace,
A silly wiggle lights up the space.

When evening falls, the laughter fades,
But the memories of joy still cascade.
In fragile greens, there's much to find,
In their sunny world, they're always kind.

## Harvesting Happiness in Close Quarters

In a cozy pot, a tomato spins,
Wiggling around as the laughter begins.
Carrots peek out, each with a grin,
Sharing stories of how they've been.

Herbs chat softly, brewing their tea,
While peppers joke about being spicy and free.
In this tiny world, friendship's the key,
Planting joy in a pot, a sight to see.

Basil dances in the gentle breeze,
Sunlight trickles in—such moments please!
With roots entwined, camaraderie grows,
Who knew that veggies had such great shows?

When harvest time comes, they cheer with delight,
Together they feast, what a silly sight!
In tiny confines, they've found their fate,
A joyful banquet upon their plate!

## Dreams Unfurled in Living Clay

Within this vessel, dreams take flight,
A sprout of lettuce, oh what a sight!
Beneath the soil, a world untold,
Exciting tales of green and gold.

Radishes snicker, 'We're so round!'
'If only we'd grow taller from the ground!'
Chives with their whispers often jest,
'In life's crescendo, we're simply the best!'

A little pea pod's feeling grand,
Huddled with friends, they form a band.
Together they sing of sunshine and rain,
Wishing for laughter, never for pain.

As blossoms appear, a sight so divine,
They swirl and gather over dinner's design.
From seed to supper, each tale is spun,
In clay they bloom, oh what fun has begun!

## The Canvas of Nature's Confinement

Colorful petals in a crowded maze,
Poppies and daisies in delicate praise.
A tulip in red, a dandelion wild,
In this canvas of green, nature's child.

Florals giggle with petals so bright,
"How do you bloom? It's a curious sight!"
Each leaf has a story it joyfully tells,
While roots shake hands and weave their spells.

Cacti roll their eyes, 'We're tough and we thrive,'
'While you softies just push and strive!'
But laughter erupts as blooms gather round,
In this pot of joy, pure merriment found!

When the sun dips low and the stars come out,
All live in harmony; that's what it's about.
A quirky testament to a life so clever,
In boundless humor, we flourish together!

## Colors of Life in Glazed Enclosure

In a shiny pot, colors burst forth,
Blues and yellows, they've shared their worth.
Pink blooms waltz while greens sway along,
Singing sweet tunes, the garden's a song.

"Let's have a party!" the herbs shout with glee,
As the garlic claps hands, quite merrily.
Potted delight, it's a lively affair,
Joy sprinkles laughter into the air.

Chilies with swagger, wearing a grin,
Say 'We spice it up, let the fun begin!'
A pot full of colors, such funny sights,
Nature's parade in the warm golden lights.

When it's dinner time, those colors unite,
Dancing on plates, oh what a delight!
In the glazed enclosure, they've made their stand,
With humor and love, they've bloomed, hand in hand.

## The Art of Patience in a Ceramic Shell

Inside my little pot, I wait,
Waiting for the sun, my mate.
Growing slow, I dream of green,
In this cozy space, I'm keen.

With roots that wiggle, twist, and twine,
I ponder if I'll reach the vine.
Each raindrop feels like a dance,
In my tiny world, I take a chance.

The squirrels stop by, they tease me so,
'You'll grow big, eventually, though!'
I giggle softly with each sprout,
Who knew that waiting's what it's about?

So here I sit, with pot in hand,
Comedic waits, not what I planned.
But laughter blooms beneath the sun,
In my ceramic home, I've just begun.

## Embraced by Earth, Sheltered by Sky

Here beneath the starry glare,
I peek at clouds without a care.
With soil hugs that feel just right,
I giggle in the soft moonlight.

The ants parade, they march like knights,
While bugs zoom by on buzzing flights.
Each worm whispers a secret cheer,
In my safe nook, there's nothing to fear.

Daydreams sprout from every crack,
In my snug place, there's no lack.
The sun wraps me in golden rays,
I chuckle at these blooming days.

The wind sings soft, a silly song,
Telling tales of where I belong.
Together we'll grow, day by day,
In this earthen home, I laugh and play.

## Crisply Wrapped in Leafy Dreams

Wrapped up tight, like a gift to see,
Whispers of leaves, just you and me.
In my leafy blanket, soft and bright,
I wiggle around with sheer delight.

Oh, how the sunlight tickles me,
In this delightful green spree.
Underneath my leafy dome,
I chuckle with the breeze, my home.

Did I just hear a beetle laugh?
What a silly little gaffe!
With every munch and chew they make,
I ponder on a tiny break.

Nature's circus, such a show,
With all my friends, I laugh and grow.
Crisp and fresh, in dreams I twirl,
Who thought a leaf could spin such a whirl?

## Whispers of Growth in Pedestal Pools

In my pedestal of earthy fun,
I listen to the giggles of the sun.
With each new sprout, I shake a leg,
In this growth game, I want to beg.

The puddles form a laugh parade,
While raindrops play, I'm unafraid.
Each splash is like a hearty cheer,
In my pot, there's joy to steer.

Frogs croak tales of who they eat,
As critters dance upon my feet.
In this pot, wild dreams ignite,
Each silly bounce makes the world feel right.

With whispers soft from roots below,
I chuckle as my petals grow.
Here's to life, strange and spryly spun,
In pedestal pools, we laugh as one.

www.ingramcontent.com/pod-product-compliance
Lightning Source LLC
Chambersburg PA
CBHW070310120526
44590CB00017B/2614